The Baboons of Hada

ERIC ORMSBY was born in Atlanta, Georgia. A distinguished scholar in the field of Islamic thought, he received a doctorate in Near Eastern Studies from Princeton University and taught at McGill University, Montreal for twenty years, where from 1996 he was Professor and Director of the Institute of Islamic Studies. In 2005 he moved to London where he took up a post as Senior Research Associate at the Institute of Ismaili Studies. In addition to his extensive writing on Classical Arabic literature and Islamic thought, and his translations from Arabic and Persian, he has published six poetry collections and is an essayist and reviewer and the author of two critical works on poetry and translation.

ERIC ORMSBY

The Baboons of Hada

Selected Poems

CARCANET

First published in Great Britain in 2011 by

Carcanet Press Limited
Alliance House
Cross Street
Manchester M2 7AQ

Copyright © Eric Ormsby 1990, 1992, 1997, 2001, 2004, 2007, 2011

Poems originally published in *Time's Covenant: New and Selected Poems*
(Windsor, ON: Biblioasis, 2007) are reproduced
by kind permission of the publisher.

A CIP catalogue record for this book is available from the British Library

ISBN 978 1 84777 066 0

The publisher acknowledges financial assistance from Arts Council England

Supported by
ARTS COUNCIL
ENGLAND

Typeset by XL Publishing Services, Tiverton
Printed and bound in England by SRP Ltd, Exeter

Contents

III

IV

for Irena

Listen,
As best you are able catch the small notes,
A sparrow's chatter behind a blackbird's tune,
A semiquaver in the voice, segregating false from true,
A mandolin shedding pale coins through the leaves.

Marius Kociejowski, 'Dinu Lipatti Plays
Chopin's Sonata in B Minor'

Origins

I wanted to go down to where the roots begin,
To find words nested in their almond skin,
The seed-curls of their birth, their sprigs of origin.

At night the dead set words upon my tongue,
Drew back their coverings, laid bare the long
Sheaths of their roots where the earth still clung.

I wanted to draw their words from the mouths of the dead,
I wanted to strip the coins from their heavy eyes,
I wanted the rosy breath to gladden their skins.

All night the dead remembered their origins,
All night they nested in the curve of my eyes,
And I tasted the savour of their seed-bed.

I

After Becquer

The dark swallows will come back again
But we, my darling, where will we be then?
The dark swallows will come back again

And build their nests beneath the balconies.
And we, will we be less than these
Flitting wings that hide our histories?

Will we be less than these
Covert-creatures of the faithful spring?
I feel the fury of each little wing

That brings the season of our hope again.
The black swallows fly and build upon
The secret nests they left us when

They flew in autumn. When they come again,
Darling, we'll be gone,
And long forgotten, but oblivion

Will give the swallows twigs to build upon.

Our Spiders

Naši pavouci…

Our spiders are theatrical.
Their webs are glitzy and their spinnerets
Sequin the silk they unspool as they spin.
They step processional as majorettes,
Each pedipalp held firm against each shin,
Their swivel-eyes fur-bristled and octagonal.

Our spiders are most musical:
Their eight silk glands echo calliopes
That pedal, as they strum their tender strings,
Chromatic and Minervan melodies
That quiver on the hornet's captive wings
Like Palestrina at his most polyphonal.

Our spiders are convivial,
With intersecting webs of bonhomie;
They pool the vagaries of katydids,
They interlace to ward off anomie;
And when an ageing spider hits the skids
She's invited to a lunch that's terminal.

Some say our spiders are maniacal;
That paranoia complicates their orbs;
That mutterings among them multiply
And that they snare each other with veiled barbs;
That the trapdoor spider gorged on caddis fly
Considers the tarantula fanatical.

I say our spiders are rhapsodical
Eremites of tactile syllables.
They weave a sisterhood where vocal silk
Labyrinths their mystic mandibles.
Gorgias must have sipped a spider's milk.
Like him they shimmer-loom their vocables:
Our spiders are both naked and rhetorical.

Microcosm

The proboscis of the drab grey flea
Is mirrored in the majesty
Of the elephant's articulated trunk. There's a sea
In the bed-mite's dim orbicular eye.
Pinnacles crinkle when the mountain-winged, shy
Moth wakes up and stretches for the night.
Katydids enact the richly patterned light
Of galaxies in their chirped and frangible notes.
The smallest beings harbour a universe
Of telescoped similitudes. Even those Rocky Mountain goats
Mimic Alpha Centauri in rectangular irises
Of cinnabar-splotched gold. Inert viruses
Replicate the static of red-shifted, still chthonic
Cosmoi. Terse
As the listened brilliance of the pulsar's bloom
The violaceous mildew in the corner room
Proliferates in Mendelian exuberance.
There are double stars in the eyes of cyclonic
Spuds shovelled and spaded up. The dance
Of Shiva is a cobble-soled affair –
Hobnails and flapping slippers on the disreputable stair.
Yggdrasils
Germinate on Wal-Mart windowsills.

Conch Shell

1

The conch shell on our kitchen counter leans
Sideways on its spiky, flaring lip,
Displaying a pinkish, petal-like interior.
The outer shell, much grittier,
Still has its papery membrane, a brown caul
Flaking away in tatters. This reminds us
That our shell is not mere ornament
But once housed some unappealing pale
Worm or slug-like being;
One of those slippery, spittle-
Mantled creatures who construct, laborious
In secretion, such begonia-plush
Palaces of glory.

Shells are paradoxical the way they draw
The eye, and then the fingertips, inside.
When we peek inside the conch shell,
There is a sloping balustrade of faint
Pink before the darkness, almost like a bare
Shoulder glimpsed briefly in a window-frame.
When we look within, the final light
Dissolves in shadow, just as once we peered
Upward to where the staircase of our childhood
Spiralled into the dark.

2

The conch is the trumpet of solemn festivals
And its pinnacle – auger-threaded,
Spire-sleek, piquant as lance-
Tip or the brass casque of a khan –
Scalpels the roughened currents asunder.
But the russet life that hides inside,
Whose flesh tastes good in broths,
Flinches from the light.

The secret fabricator of itself,
Refusing to be known
By anything beyond the dawn-pink
Shell that houses and articulates
Its lithe inhabitant –
How that small crawling diffidence,
The slime-wreathed animal that flows,
A pygmy to its own magnificence,
Inches ocean runnels, seraphically akimbo!
This recluse with a flare for ostentation,
Glabrous and glistening, secure in glory
That it secretes but cannot see,
Emblems a self in its configuration.

3

I've seen conchs docked and husked,
Stripped of their calcareous splendour, plump
Amorphous things, arching, like tongues
Torn from mouths or some hidden
Shapelessness of desire drawn into the sun.
I've seen the unrecognisable architect
Of itself marketed in dripping baskets,
Leaving behind nothing but the pale
Pulsing of remembered oceans
In the veiled shell's proclamatory lip.

Starfish

The stellar sea-crawler, maw
Concealed beneath, with offerings of
Prismed crimson now darkened, now like
The smile of slag, a thing made rosy
As poured ingots, or suddenly dimmed –

I appreciate the studious labour
Of your rednesses, the scholarly fragrance
Of your sex. To mirror tidal drifts
The light ripples across or to enhance darkness
With palpable tinctures, dense as salt.

You crumple like a puppet's fist
Or erect, bristling, your tender luring barbs.
Casual abandon, like a dropped fawn glove.
Tensile symmetries, like a hawk's claw.

You clutch the seafloor.

You taste what has fallen.

Ant-Lion

Beneath your shoe soles an illusion smooths
The loose lank sandgrains into cavities
So exquisitely cocked that if you tease
Their edges with a straw the funnel seethes

Suddenly under to blank avalanche.
I saw a plodding ant's insouciance
Topple it over in a scramble-dance
Down down down into the clench

Of the ant-lion. Chaplinesque
Assassin of the sand, snug predator,
Larval hunter with a gladiator
Lunge of needle-mandibles, burlesque

Doodlebug, we called it, to domesticate
Terror made tiny, mayhem minusculed.
Below our eyes its drab precision ruled
Lilliputian worlds with silicate

Strategies, glint-facades of fright.
And sometimes when the ambushed day
Bleedingly withdrew to slumberous grey,
I heard my heartbeat striking in the night.

In dream sometimes the cliff-brink of the world,
That zigzag fracture of hurt porcelain
That leads beyond the darkness of the brain,
Funnels and shimmies, woozies to a hurled

Helter-skelter of ankles and shrill clothes
Upended, and we paw, in a fierce crawl,
Bare air, eyes dragged upward as our bodies fall,
Somersaulted, with heart-stoppered mouths.

And if our fall were only infinite,
If falling were our pleasure and our grace,
If our momentum obviated place,
If our descent were indeterminate...!

What taloned nightmare grips us in the wild
Spiral of sleep? What ripped awakening?
What busy, greedy, inconspicuous thing?
What barely fledged phantasm of a child?

The ant-lion shrugs aside its camouflage,
Ruthless as a consumer elbows near
With upraised boning knife to shear
Something for that deep-freeze in the garage.

In dream we flutter above everyone.
In dream we Ixion the darkened sun.
Under our shoes a pinch of sand holds night –
Darkness puppeteered by appetite.

Spider

I caught a spider sucking a drink
From the kitchen sponge. Its thirst
Disgusted me. I didn't want to know
How our requirements coincide.

Still, it was almost beautiful
As the spider stepped from the wet sponge
And swung into the pot of mint,
Where I knew
It would rest and hide and savour
The cool taste of water
In its dark mouth.

Flamingos

1

My quarrel with your quorum, Monsignor
Flamingo, is that you scant the rubicund
In favour of a fatal petal
Tint. I would rather bask
In riots of the roseate
Than measure your footfalls'
Holy protocols beside the head-
Board of a drowsy demiurge.
I think God snores in rose
Leaves of serenity, not in your
Clatter of cadaverous vermeils.

2

I find flamingos beautiful Tartuffes
Who entice as they distance me.
When they display their billiarding
Adolescent sprawl of knees I
Remember the parochial
Schoolgirls in pink cashmeres, their rosy
Kneecaps polished by novenas.

3

Flamingos have the silhouettes
Of parking meters. They have no epaulettes
And yet seem always in uniform –
Little, stilted caudillos! They swarm
In unruffled ripples of defiling pink.
They mimic ballerinas and yet stink.
Flamingos are dirty in their purity,
Blazon Venezuelas of lewd suavity.
Beneath their transcendent, back-bent

Legs flamingos are somnolent
And lubricious birds whose stiff tutus
Amuse
The spoonbills and anhingas who erect
Nests of fish skin to reflect
The imperial smut of the sky.

                    I feel a samba roll
Under my eyelids when flamingos stroll
Oceanward at sundown and clap their stubs of wings
In gawky, rank, hierophantic posturings.

4

When the Lord God created the flamingos, He
Fell into despondency. He knew
That roseate feathers on such skeletons
Elicit incredulity. He gloomed
For days, obsessive as a poet who
Discovers a covert love affair between
Obstreperous syllables and then,
Cracking grandeur from the egg of shame,
Sets these
Diametric desperadoes in a pas de deux.

5

Only in Miami is supreme
Loneliness apparent in flamingo dawn.
The squalor of the place is cruelly pink.
There are pink curtains on the lousy shacks.
The impulse to adorn deepens the nakedness.
There flamingos all the colour of a bone
Scavenge in vermilion stateliness.
Their pink flocks forage in that loneliness.

Grackle

It's hard not to like the wise-
Guy grin, the almost sarcastic chatter
Of the boat-tailed grackle by the Everglades
Café. He has an acrid cackle,
A cacophony of slick and klaxon cries,
With tinsel whispers like a breathy flute.

His repertoire seems meant to flatter
Us by mimicry and so exonerate
Our grosser faults, our greeds,
Our clumsy cunnings, our minute
Duplicities.

               Watch how he hops elastically
From roof-beam down to a potato chip
And shrills and wheedles while his hard claws grip
Whittled bench-rims and the slats of rails.
He strides like a chimney sweep,
Char-coloured, and yet, see:
His cinder eyes are absolute.
Cunning of hunger makes his feathers bright
In smoky lapis, iris-indigo.

Anhinga

There is a callisthenic finesse to the neck
As the poke-stick of the beak
Comes up. The neck's loop revolves,
Too sinuous to be plausible.
This neck has innuendoes of a fish,
Must writhe and must wriggle and
Must pivot in sopping
Twists, distinctively drip-dry,
Till the rough feathers regain their brackish glare.

Eel-spasms, annular
Cascades, clamber the bayberry
Over the frilled sludge where the gar
Gelatinises in its own repose.
The anhingas ogle the gorgeous sky
Over Shark River and as they gaze
Extend vespertilian
Wings, meticulous and moist.
They hold their pose.
It's almost reverential for those,
Like me, with worshipful proclivities
When these black birds spread out such wings.

O anhingas on the floodgates and the levee bridge,
You pray with nothing but water and I see
Your signatory darkness cloak the sun.

Rooter

For Tippy

I like the way the rooster lifts his feet,
So jauntily exact,
Then droops one springy yellow claw aloft
Just like a tailor gathering up a pleat.
And then there are those small surprising lilts,
Both rollicking and staid,
That grace his bishop's gait,
Like a waltzer on a pair of supple stilts
Or a Russian on parade.

I like the way he swivels and then slants
His red, demented eye
To tipsy calibrations of his comb
And ogles the barnyard with a shopkeeper's stance.
Sometimes his glossy wattles shudder and bulge
As he bends his feathered ear
And listens, fixed in trance.
When drowsy grubs below the ground indulge
And then stretch up for air,

How promptly he administers his peck,
Brisk and executive,
And the careless victim flipflops in his grip!
I like the way his stubby little beak
Produces that dark, corroded croak
Like a grudging nail tugged out of stubborn wood:
No 'cock-a-doodle-doo' but *awk-a-awk!*
He yawps whenever he's in the mood
And the thirst and clutch of life are in his squawk.

Chiefly I love the delicate attention
Of the waking light that falls
Along his shimmery wings and bubbling plumes
As though light pleasured in tangerine and gentian
Or sported like some splashy kid with paints.
But Rooster forms his own cortège, gowns
Himself in marigold and shadow, flaunts
His scintillant, prismatic tints –
The poorest glory of a country town.

Watchdog and Rooster

Surveying the henhouse with profound
Vigilance, taut on his tether,
Alert in sleet as well as heatstroke weather,
Crouched, eye ajar, the farmer's hound.
The rooster, however,
Accustomed to the chuckling palaver
Of his cackleophilous concubines,
Disliked the stolid silence of the dog
Who hunched there like a stinkpot on a log
And only uttered small obsequious whines
About his master's boots at supper-time.

Let us see (the rooster mused) *if this dull mutt,*
This grovel-muzzled mongrel, this bacon-butt,
This caravan of fleas, this tick-parade,
This yap-infested bozo, slow and spayed,
Let's see, I say, if this back-alley terrier,
This rumple-bellied harrier
Of shrews and voles, of polecats and hedgehogs,
Can cut the mustard with the bigger dogs!

Rooster waited till the dog, galvanised
By gazing, nodded; then, in fowlish pantomime
He stalked across the barnyard in a trot
Until he reached a strategic spot
Below the watchdog's downward drooping ear.
He then let fly a loud chanticleer
Rawp that left the stunned hound paralysed.
The hound had never been hard
Of hearing, quite the opposite.
The clangorous crowing of the rooster, shrill pasha,
Rattled in his brainpan like a washer
On a wind-tormented pipe. He pounced.
He took the raucous rooster by the throat and trounced
Him on the barnyard till he bit
His insupportable windpipe cleanly through.

The moral of this fable still rings true:
Muzzle the watchdog when you cock-a-doodle-doo.

Craneworld

When the sandhill crane resolves
to hatch her universe, emphatic
designs impose on her angle of view.
Her innate notions are splashy but few.
The blueprint of craneworld involves
thatchiness, a prickledom of aromatic
nestnesses. It is spatulate and concave
together, and is conspicuous in fish.

In craneworld the sun is both god and slave
and the night rises in the darkness of the eye
itself.

       Frogs' voices console her cosmos lavish-
ly and there is the strong calendar of sky
southward.

       Her inwardness is spherical, grit-white,
concentric in its cadences, with gravities of light.

Cradle-Song of the Emperor Penguins

Shackleton is stranded far to the north of us,
The *Endurance* stands gripped in the fists of the ice.

The skuas have withdrawn to the Cape, the leopard
Seals laze in the sun of the Weddell Sea.

Our wives have trekked back to warm surf having laid
Their eggs on our feet to brood-hatch with our blood.

Our empresses have left us to the long night of the ice.
Like goalies we cradle tense futures on our toes,

Dandling our babes against our belly skin:
All winter we will stand in a pod of palaver

Against the winds of Erebus and shield our chicks
Under pouches of down and coverlets of quill.

In the long night of the world when the green
Krakens of the aurora writhe

We fast and hold our hunger to the wind.
Our children hatch darkly. They hug our toes for life.

My tufty chicks, my fuzz-downy bairns,
I will guard you when the leopards

Of September return. I will shield you
When the towers topple into the seas of ash.

The soot of winter night is on my tongue,
The cinders of ambushed dawn are in my eyes,

Yet I will shelter you against my belly skin
And warm your feather-weakness with heart's blood
And cradle you on the crèches of my claws.

The Egyptian Vulture

Egyptian Vultures are well known as being the least discriminating of scavengers.
W.-E. Cook, *Avian Desert Predators*

The Egyptian Vulture is the least
discriminating of the scavengers.
He sucks up eyeball juice of wildebeest
as though it were iced Bollinger.

He spreads a grey paté of rotted gnu
on a barfed-up bed of jungle turkey comb.
Raw rectum of gazelle is *cordon bleu*
yet how piously he dines, with plumed aplomb!

The stomach contents of some ripe giraffe
pleasure him more than freshly slivered truffles.
He stuffs his whole head in and you hear him laugh
as he snacks on gassy guts and belly ruffles.

Would you really call him *indiscriminate*?
True, his topknot is fouled with shit and bile
(unavoidable when you work your snout in straight
up the flyblown butt of some long-dead crocodile),

but see how he grooms himself when his chow is done:
he hangs his litigious pinions out to air,
he preens his turban till it's debonair,
he strops his beak in the Egyptian sun.

Garter Snake

The stately ripple of the garter snake
In sinuous procession through the grass
Compelled my eye. It stopped and held its head
High above the lawn, and the delicate curve
Of its slender body formed a letter S –
For 'serpent', I assume, as though
Diminutive majesty obliged embodiment.

The garter snake reminded me of those
Cartouches where the figure of a snake
Seems to suggest the presence of a god
Until, more flickering than any god,
The small snake gathered glidingly and slid,
But with such cadence to its rapt advance
That when it stopped once more to raise its head,
It was stiller than the stillest mineral
And when it moved again, it moved the way
A curl of water slips along a stone
Or like the ardent progress of a tear
Till, deeper still, it gave the rubbled grass
And the dull hollows where its ripple ran
Lithe scintillas of exuberance,
Moving the way a chance felicity
Silvers the whole attention of the mind.

The Baboons of Hada

The baboons of Hada love the heights.
High places let them contemplate
The sordid valleys they have left behind.
Along the scalded stones blue lizards lie,
Flatten themselves or pump their beaded throats.
But the baboons of Hada are aloof.
The baboons know the indifference of peaks;
Even their antics are deliberate;
Their skipping over crags has stateliness.

I like the way the baboons of the heights
Have colonised the coldest pinnacle,
Have softened and made stoical and sly
The summits where five stringy crows still wheel,
Have humourised abysses, made crevasses
Comical, vaudevilleaned the avalanche.
Now the sweet sisters groom their brothers' braids,
Old aunties coif the moustaches of nieces;
Their bright fastidious molars crackle mites.

And all the while one Abrahamic ape,
The dominant, the doge of his troupe,
Hunkers heraldic on a lip of stone.
His silvery Hamitic sideburns fluff
In the breezes of the heights. He shuts both eyes.
The patriarch of Hada shuts his eyes
And all around is sibilance and gust.
The scavenger baboons, consanguineous,
Plump down on their buttocks in the calm.

A sense of fullness rises with the dusk.
Five crows still quarrel at contested scraps
But the lord of foragers is throned in peace
Amid the frisky chittering of his kids.
The baboons wait until the rocks of heights
Become supernal in the full moon's light.
At nightfall the baboons of Hada sit
In chuckling circles where they contemplate
The radiant bottom of the risen moon.

Lichens

Between the stones, by the sea's edge,
And in sheltered hollows of the rock,
Flat lichens cling. Their surfaces are grey,
Dry and crinkly. Some are cracked and sharp
Or flake away like weathered paint in strips.
They survive the cold light and the spray
Torn from the North Atlantic. The way they clasp
And cover the rocks seems to signify
Inconspicuous courage and tenacity. But
At evening they gleam bleakly in exact
Configurations and their order is fiercer
Than the sea's: their drab arabesques
Look splotchy, rust-wept or scaly as dead bark;
Far-off they're starlike, spiky as galaxies.
Like us they clutch and grip their chilly homes
And the wind defines their possibilities.

Milkweed

The milkweed with its stringent silk
Erect in October when the long blades lie
Burnished to glistening under a dwindling sky,
And the trees have the accents of things about to die,
Startled my glance, the way the tressed and milk-
Bright strands of its hidden diadem
Peep from the knobbed and gathered pods.
A field of milkweed, where each black stem
Juts from the cold earth, catches the sun
At its palest declination. Spun
Inside themselves, concealed in the husk
Of their future, the folds of the seeds
Are pleated upon themselves, are wound
The way a woman wraps a shawl at dusk
Over her shoulders. The weeds
Are populous. They column neglected ground.
Tassel and toss the smudged air of the fall.
And from a little distance the stalks grow tall
And shattered, porch and peristyle
Of some yet undiscovered ruin. Meanwhile,
At the breeze's twitch, the seeds rise
Upon the air, are lofted, puffed, they float
In the sunset, flitter like white butterflies
And inhabit all your sight. With no note
Struck they lilt on the wind, speckle the slope,
Already winter-darkened, with small swales of hope.

Skunk Cabbage

The skunk cabbage with its smug and opulent smell
Opens in plump magnificence near the edge
Of garbage-strewn canals, or you see its shape
Arise near the wet roots of the marsh.
How vigilant it looks with its glossy leaves
Parted to disclose its bruised insides,
That troubled purple of its blossom!

It always seemed so squat, dumpy and rank,
A noxious efflorescence of the swamp,
Until I got down low and looked at it.

Now I search out its blunt totemic shape
And bow when I see its outer stalks
Drawn aside, like the frilly curtains of the ark,
For the foul magenta of its gorgeous heart.

Mullein

A pleasure secret and austere.

Archibald Lampman, 'In November'

And mossy scabs of the wormfence, and heaped stones,
and elder and mullen and pokeweed.

Walt Whitman, 'Song of Myself'

1

Death is a kind of opportunity,
Deprivation possibility,
Where this weed strikes its root.
The mullein's infinitesimal black seeds
Crave for vacancy to germinate.
It startles me to see it colonnade
Defoliated roadsides and in June, impressed,
I round its plush and nettled obelisk.
From winter-clenched rosettes it pokes, man-high,
And grows big and green where other green things die.

All verticality, the mullein has a plumed
Columnar stature with up-curled
Leaves that stand out from its stalk
Like stiffened shavings on a whittled stick.
And from these curlicue-attentive leaves
The raceme of the mullein with
Its padded shaft ascends, a quilted
Polygon. And all along the raceme's
Naked length, little flowers appear,
Yellow-petalled to the pinnacle.

2

In vinyl bedooms of cold-eyed hotels,
When I'm unable to imagine home
And when my own grim turn of mind
Depopulates familiarity
And nothing can people my sleep again,
I sometimes glimpse a mullein by the weed-
Whacked border of the parking lot,
Invisible though so conspicuous
Beyond the stuttering whiteness of the flood-
Lit asphalt, or poplaring a sewer-pipe,

And I like the way, from what nobody else
Would bother with, it sends a column up.
I like that it domesticates
Small desolations and that it pinches place
From peripheries where places cannot be
And that its wispy petal sweetens haggardness.
I like out of how little mullein makes
A shade. So it can mollify the bleak
Suite, the long hours of the night coming on,
That lurid doily with its Gideon.

3

If I were given to apostrophe,
I'd say to mullein, 'Poke up, sprout, extend!
Be opportunistic, shrewd, exuberant.
Along storm gutters or the rims
Of gaudy troughs of algae-ruffled seepage,
Still be gauntly numerous, redeem the brink,
Sentinel the emptiness seraphically.
Drive your root in nihil till it spout
And flutter out, to pleasure flies and bees,
Your thin yellow flowers of astonishment.'

Live Oak, with Bromeliads

The live oak tufted with bromeliads
By the salt lagoon looks almost scarred.
Airplants bristle on its grey
Limbs like knotted sprigs of surgeon's thread.
In sprawling notches of the canopy
Spanish moss dangles in snarled clusters
While the long sunshine of Miami's winter
Lends it a gloss of fractured malachite.

But nothing could be less wounded than this oak.
Its knuckled roots infiltrate the dank
Marsh of the hammock, they drink the sand
Riddled by land-crabs to a moon-pocked surface.
And look:
            Like praying candles in a smoky shrine
Set up to honour the salt god of the marsh
The ranked branches embrace their parasites.

II

The Crossing

1

She saw the granite hills of Newfoundland.
Icebergs impressed her with their hiddenness.
A twelve-year-old in pigtails, thin and plain,
Nursing her smarting knowledge by the iron
Rail of the great ship
Ploughing west.

                Grandmother, life was still
Before you then. The year was 1881.
Questions of birth and 'station' already
Riddled you but in the grey
Fish-oily waters of the Grand Banks,
You saw murres and gannets, birdlime-morticed rock,
And the way the tenant birds peered from their crevices,
Row upon row in rowdy harmony
Like choristers arrayed for the grand chorale,
Seemed almost a parody of paradise:
The disparate in unison, a public peace,
The serried dovecotes of the raucous blessed,
A world where everyone had found a place.

2

As a child I peeked into her diary
Of the crossing. Now it's lost. I popped
The frail gilt lock and recognised
The classic copperplate of her dead hand.
A factual account. Spotting a pod
Of whales. The way the galley smelled.
The look of the sun at sea. Prosaically
Her every breakfast registered in neat
Detail. She had already learned to hide
All that she felt; her legacy
Was already handed down to us as if it were

Precarious porcelain, worn ivory,
The heirloom bauble of her secrecy.

3

She shepherded her secrets into Tennessee,
Those hills of abnegation, those
Refusing fields, the bitter
Immemorial drudgery. Rugby,
Tennessee, was one of those
Brutal utopias America loves:
In winter chilblains and in summer dust.
The rough-adzed privy stank and in
The sullen windowframes, Tennysonian
Bluebottles tossed without one smidgeon of
The lovely music of his desolation.

One day, her father, boilermaker's son
From Westminster with gentlemanly longings,
Cut their new surname
Into the lower pane of a parlour window
Where I spotted it a century afterwards:
MILMOW, with Falstaffian swagger scratched
Into glass, as though it could not change
Or be effaced, as though it stood
Unalterable to slander or the scuff of time.
And in January, in the stoveless
Pantry, every windowsill was rimmed with ice,
Like children's eyes with all their tears
Frozen inside them.

4

When you surprised your mother in a still,
Despondent mood, her eyes so far away,
You thought to say to her, *Maman,*
À quoi penses-tu? Knowing that if you spoke
In mother-French she was likelier to reply.

And Maman looked at you and gave a sigh,
À bien des choses, ma petite, à bien des choses!
– the question and reply a ritual
remembered into long old age.

                                        And evenings, as she
Wound her hair upon her head, I'd hear
Her whisper, *Notre père qui es aux cieux...*
She enunciated each pure phrase until I felt
The distant winter nights of Tennessee,
The firelight of their voices, comfortable
Hubbub, the intertwine of anecdote
And twig-crumple, the whistle of the seethed
Sap between the pondered pauses of their
Voices – ceremonious,
Half-whispering, a stately colloquy
Unremarkable except for cadences:
People talk at night so musically
To the firelight's sly accompaniment.
And if I listened to her reminisce,
The vanished voices of her sisters
Came to me again with all
The soft fiery pleasures of the hearth.

5

I feel a tenderness of memory,
Grandmother, as though I heard your voice again
And the great sea were both our memory now.
And I will cross into your history
The way adopted children peek behind
The secrets of their surnames to discern
Darkness after darkness of the past.
And maybe it must always be just so
Whenever we touch the childhood of the dead.

Getting Ready for the Night

When Grandma combed her fine white hair at night
Until it toppled to her shoulder blades
In startling cascades, bright-angel-winged,
She looked like Milton's seraph at the gate
Of paradise: sovereign, ingenuous and stern.
I marvelled in the ripples of her hair
The teasing and impertinent lamplight touched.
But, 'Won't you clip my toenails for me now?'
She said and then, with a stoic sigh,
'It's hard to be so old, so incapable.'

I didn't want to touch her pallid foot
And yet, it felt astonishing when her left
Foot nestled in my clasp and I began
Scissoring the wrinkled horn of nail
With snipping shears until the pale
Translucencies of toenail ribboned off.
Her sole felt warm in my deft paw.
And suddenly I could appreciate
Grandma being mortal, one who sheds
Skin and nails and all integuments.

But then she twined
And spooled her colourless flat hair
About accustomed fingers into supple
Braids
          And I was baffled in the tenderness
Her silk-shaded light winked down on both of us.

I snipped her toenails
Evenly. Together we prepared her
For the night. Together we made sure
That shorn and braided, she would enter into
The encirclements of darkness just beyond
The pooled, penurious
Empire of the lamp.

The Suitors of my Grandmother's Youth

At dusk on Sabbath afternoons the slow-
Voiced suitors came, with awkward hat brims in
Their field-burred hands. They tipped themselves
On the very brinks of the Sunday chairs.
Their napes were fiery under their collar starch.
The knees of their blue serge suits looked rubbed and smooth.

Fireflies would be winking then, across the lawns.
Under the hedge, like small and sleepy stars
Witnessed through mist, they glittered and went out.
And everywhere, lilac would spire in June
Its chaste and promissory fragrance. Her
Sisters broke off sprays and clasped them
With half-ironic passion to their throats.
The boys were mute, traded long-suffering
Conspiratorial looks. On speechless
Strolls their beaux would hand to them
Desperate fistfuls of wild violets.
All their futures still appeared
Benign with promise, all their loves
Still hovered before the transactions of the blood.

Two Views of My Grandfather's Courting Letters

Quidve mali fuerat nobis non esse creatis?

Lucretius

1

So here is where it all began, in these
limp prevarications and apologies!
I recognise Grandfather's courting voice too well,
its little stylistic flinches: 'It would be swell
if you held me still *Your Affectionate Friend...*'
he coaxes and then, abjectly, near the end,
'Don't judge me so hard, Miss Juliet, despite
the jackass I made of myself last Saturday night.'

I could be reading letters I wrote myself,
except that these have lain ninety-four years on a shelf.
These are his courtship letters which she saved,
locked in a metal strongbox, though she raved
against his 'great foolishness' all her long old age.
She kept his memory bright in the soft claw of her rage.

Reading these letters I want to shout:
'Grandfather, stop! Fold up the paper! Switch out
the lamp on the supper table. Put back the quill
pen, whittled to a nib, in its snug inkwell
and tuck the unfranked stamps in the escritoire.
Cross your wedding date from the calendar.
Sidestep the meagre pleasures, the great pains, to come –
the horror of a wedding bed that left you numb,
the brusque rebuffs or, at best, the grudged embrace
in conjugal obligation to prolong the human race.
I beg of you – I, wiser by nothing but distance –
confer on us, out of your countrified extravagance
and gentle hospitality
(my single memory of you,
kind whiskers and a kiss),
confer on us

with what you fail to write,
the pure gift not to be.'

2

Holding his old letters I can see
how he copied each word out painstakingly –
a schoolboy polishing his copperplate.
All his hopes are still inviolate.
And I would not have it otherwise at last.
I would not soften the horror of the past.
But see, between the salvaged paragraphs,
the clumsy jauntiness, the staves and staffs,
laborious penmanship, with curlicues,
affected to impress and to amuse.

The penning of these letters on the page
fissures the time between, a saxifrage
stubbornness of promise. I have seen the root
pierce rock. I have seen the puny shoot
split stone where it flowers and endures.
Not-being-born appears so pure
but my grandfather's clumsy courtliness
shyly jollies nothingness,
embarrasses as it redeems.
I fold his letters back along their seams
and shelter them in sandalwood.

And I will say, *Write us in the book of life,*
Grandfather, inscribe us there for good.

In the Abrahamic lamp
of a Georgia twilight, my grandfather picks up his pen
and writes,

> *Dearest Juliet,*
> *Will you be mine?*

Adages of a Grandmother

Grandmother said to me, 'Keep thyself
Unspotted from the world.' She spoke in quotes.
I got the feeling that she had rehearsed
All her admonitions as a child,
For when she issued them to me she grew
Solemn and theatrical. I knew
She tasted in her words some sweet
Indissoluble flavour of the past; but even more,
As though at eighty-five or eighty-six
She stood still in the parlour of her recitation
– a plain, studious girl with long brown braids
(I have the portraits of her as a child)
– and spoke her lessons for approving guests.
Such touches of girlishness accompanied
Her adages. And then she gave me dimes
For so many lines of Shakespeare memorised.
For 'The quality of mercy...' I was paid
A quarter, and at tea I gave her guests
A dollar's worth of Shakespeare with their toast.
'All the world's a stage,' she reminded me.

Only armed with an adage might I sally forth.
'A foolish son's his mother's grief,' she thought.
The world was scriptural and stratified.
It held raw veins of wisdom in its side,
Like the Appalachians when we journeyed north.
She sat in the front seat of the Buick, hair-net drawn
Over her white hair coiled in a dignified bun,
Her straw-beflowered hat alert and prim.
From the back seat I'd study her, my grim
Grandmother, with her dictatorial
Chin, her gold-rimmed spectacles ablaze with all
The glory of the common highway where
Field daisies spoke to her in doctrinaire
Confidential accents of the master plan
Confided to grandmothers by the Son of Man.

Wisdom was talismanic and opaque;
Could be carried in a child's small fist
Like the personal pebble I fished out of the lake.
And whenever I stepped outside she kissed
My head and armed me with a similitude.
Beyond the screen door, past the windowsill,
The bright earth rang with providence until
Even the wise ants at my shoe-tips moved
In dark amazements of exactitude
And the small dusty sparrows swooped innumerably.

I write this on the sun-porch of the house
Where she lay, an invalid, in her last years.
And I'm abashed to realise I blamed
Her stiffness and her stubborn uprightness
For much that happened to me afterward.
Now I look through the window where she looked
And see the sunlight on the windowsill
And wonder what it signifies,
For now I barely recognise
Her world outside, as though sunlight effaced
Not only human features but their memory.
Her adages are all scattered in my head
(*Neither a borrower nor a lender be*)
and I cannot think for thinking of the dead
(*Go to the ant, thou sluggard,*
consider her ways, and be wise.)
I cannot read the world now with her eyes
(*A wise son maketh a glad father but*
A foolish son is the heaviness of his mother!)
And I, who used to blame her so,
Now rummage in my pockets for
A nickel's worth of wisdom for my kids.

Hand-Painted China

The slender cake plates had such fiery rims.
They caught the lazy radiance
Of afternoons like torch-
Light from a tomb. The old
Roses opened to my eyes
Their bold, embellished centres
Where a soft darkness had
Been stippled in. They drew down
My gaze until I felt
Labyrinthed in sweetness like a bee.

My great-aunts painted these.
The hesitant brush strokes on their
Undersides read '1893'.
The greenness of their china does not fade
But witnesses an opulence the more forlorn
For being without issue. The pinks
And gilts, the ravelled petals
Blowsy with magenta, importune
The fingers to partake of them.

These were the gravy boats of plenteous
Expectation, the creamers rich with dream;
These were the banquet platters, these
The hard yet fragile saucers, of trousseaux.
These were the festive dishes no one used.
Now they snag the curious
Light of afternoons
In magisterial shadow
Like a pharaoh's mouth.

Here,
In the lovingly abrasive, gently gritted
Impasto of hand-painted surfaces
That resist, like skin, with almost plush aplomb,
I feel some embodiment of all
Their expectations had the right to claim.
I feel their tentative fingertips touch mine.

Finding a Portrait of the Rugby Colonists,
My Ancestors Among Them

It is as if you held them all, as God
Must have held them when He made their
Mouths, their shoulders, their irreplaceable
Eyes. It is as if their world were in your hands,
Here, in this rectangular beechwood frame
With the brown paper backing that complains like flame
With crackling annoyance when you tug the wire,
Bright-twisted, that sustained it on some wall.
There is a Godlike feeling to encompass so
On a flat, embrittled print their many lives,
Though only in effacement can you hope
To sustain their least regard.

                              To enter this
Beech-embrasured instant when a lens
With curatorial dispassion caught
Their momentary countenances asks
The modesty of trustful ignorance.
And though you cannot know them, yet you feel
Bone-closeness to their lives.

                              Tell me, if you had been
The God who shaped their cheekbones
And their brows, the dignified alertness
Of their ears, their ceremonial and
Formal smiles, their throats the patience of a
May sun mottled with its little dabs of luminance,
The fingers curved on Bibles or on canes,
The feet in their black-thonged propriety
Of dainty boots or strenuous clodhoppers,
Would you, for a world,
Have let them tumble into
Nothingness and seen their strong hearts rot,
Or would you have raised them up again,
The way you rouse a sleeper or a child?

A Freshly Whitewashed Room

I am sitting in the bedroom where Grandmother
Entered Calvary, where her halting breath
Prayed for the stiff-laced curtains to puff out.
I am in the sunny bedroom where she lay
So long ago, tortoised in a cast
From chin to groin. How the pallid sweat
Fled from her flesh and smarted, made her
Itch with agony while I would read
The Life of Stonewall Jackson in a high
Annunciatory voice. Unknowingly I was
Her tongue of doom. The downfall of the South
Was in her bandaged bones where Stonewall bled
Tragical as Hector although not
Heel-dragged around the city gates
But fusilladed by his own smoke-staggered men.

And she would sweat and blink in the lamp
Near where I'm sitting now, though
Early sunshine pours in from the east
And the walls are freshly whitewashed
Till they fairly blaze.
Is there a sickroom sweetness just behind this new
White wall, a troubled coughing in the wainscoting
Where field mice cache their stores? Are there echoes
Of her outcries in the dismantled fixtures?

Sometimes I think the sufferings of the old
Make heroes look ridiculous.
Sometimes I think to bring down Ilion
Was easier than to guide the bitter spoon
At medicine time to the reluctant lip.

And when the heavy book sagged in my hands
And I would nod off in the bedside chair,
'Honey,' she'd say to me, 'go over that page once more.
I need the fortitude of good example now.'
Each caisson-jolt and bivouac emboldened her.
She grappled her pain like an antagonist.

Yet, when I read out loud to her,
It felt as if my voice
Were wearing her away
And inching her into that history
She always so clamoured for.
With every word I read she seemed to me
Some punished stone an ocean works upon,
Lapping around her till it covered her
Down to the bare bedrock it rubbed away.

My Mother in Old Age

As my mother ages and becomes
Ever more fragile and precarious,
Her hands dwindle under her rings
And the freckled skin at her throat
Gathers in tender pleats like some startled fabric.
The blue translucence of her veins gives
The texture of her skin an agate gleam
And the dark-blue, almost indigo
Capillaries of her cheeks and forehead
Resemble the gentle roots
Of cuttings of violets
In sheltered jars.

         I love her now more urgently
Because there is an unfamiliar and relentless
Splendour in her face that terrifies me.

        'Oh, don't prettify decrepitude,'
She demands. 'Don't lie!
Don't make old age seem so *ornamental!*'

And yet, she abets her metamorphosis,
Invests herself in voluminous costume
Jewels and shrill polyesters

        – ambitious as a moth
To mime the dangerous leaf on which she rests.

Childhood House

For my brother Alan

After our mother died, her house, our
Childhood house, disclosed
All its deterioration to our eyes.
While living she had screened us from, or we hadn't seen,
The termite-nibbled floorboards and the rotting beams,
The wounded stucco hidden by shrubbery, the frayed
Unpredictable wiring and the clanking labour
Of the hot-water line into the discoloured
Tub; the fixtures in the dining room
Skewed and malfunctioning.

                                 I remember thinking with a
Swarm of confusion that this was the true state
Of our childhood now; this house of dilapidated girders
Eaten away at the base. Somehow I had assumed
That the past stood still, in perfected effigies of itself,
And that what we had once possessed remained our possession
Forever, and that at least the past, our past, our child-
Hood, waited, always available, at the touch of a nerve,
Did not deteriorate like the untended house of an
Ageing mother, but stood in pristine perfection, as in
Our remembrance. I see that this isn't so, that
Memory decays like the rest, is unstable in its essence,
Flits, occludes, is variable, sidesteps, bleeds away, eludes
All recovery; worse, is not what it seemed once, alters
Unfairly, is not the intact garden we remember, but
Instead, speeds away from us backwards terrifically
Until when we pause to touch that sun-remembered
Wall, the stones are friable, crack and sift down,
And we could cry at the fierceness of that velocity
If our astonished eyes had time.

Dicie Fletcher

Whene'er, along the ivory disks, are seen,
The filthy footsteps of the dark gangrene;
When caries comes, with stealthy pace to throw
Corrosive ink spots on those banks of snow –
Brook no delay, ye trembling, suffering fair,
But fly for refuge to the dentist's care.

Solyman Brown, *Dentologia: A Poem on*
the Diseases of the Teeth (1833), Canto Four

Πεῖρεν ὀδόντων

Homer, *Iliad* xvi, 405

'I have a horror of unconsciousness,' she said.
She refused the nitrous oxide mixed with oxygen
(that still was new in 1881).
'Let me come clear-eyed unto Calvary,'
Dicie Fletcher, teacher of Classics, said,
hands braced against chintz armrests while she watched
Dr Diore's lancing eye,
cool blue sun in incandescent sky,
assay each tooth-tap as he inch-
wormed nearer, nearer and still
nearer to that flinching place
where her sick tooth pulsed with pain.

'Would you reduce me to the mere *insensible*,'
she remembered, now, to her horror, having said.
'I tell you this, I disapprove of all
nepenthe. True propriety
must objurgate Lethean balm.'
O now, how she cursed those chill
Ciceronian cadences of hers!

The bad tooth
Seemed to shrink back like a guilty thing.
'They do some tiptop things these days
with hippopotamus,' Dr Diore drawled.
'It's all the thing – *ivory swaged with gold!*'

He saw the same old Dicie he had known
and hankered for for years. Since grammar school.
He shivered picturing her virginal
pale flesh swaddled inside stays and straps,
a woman barricaded behind her clothes
(and was he not the man to lay her siege?).
And Dicie looked at him, saw him up close.
His muttonchops were snarled with bloody flecks.
His jowl was peppered with old smallpox pits.
She remembered him as a small and shiftless boy –
now he'd got an office of his own, now
his thick and stubby fingers reeked of clove.

Her neckveins pounded and her temples rang.
And when Dr Diore touched the culprit tooth
She writhed against the brimming of the hurt
That wrung out fiery teardrops from her eyes.
The Cross. O the Crown of Thorns...
faded from her, faded!

Peiren odonton...

Homer was the true Evangelist.
That's what she taught her boys.
Homer did not assuage, met doom
head-on. Uncoddled by all gospels, he
only held out hard pebble-phrases
for the agonised to suck. Yes, *peiren: drove*
('Aorist, boys? Who can tell me about this verb?'
'Patroclus *drove* the spear *between the teeth* –
odonton – of Thestor, son of Enops. He
gaffed the charioteer out of his chariot
like a bullfrog on a pole.') The doctor
whooped, 'We've got it now!' ('Genitive
plural, that *omega*, boys, Homer's own
words, chilly as ivory, aloof to pain.')
She felt the bulldog bite of the clamp.
She moaned and Dr Diore stroked her brow.
'O my, my, yes, the *torture of the forceps*,' he consoled
(O how he wanted this woman, wanted her here and now!)

When a dark oak is cracked by cyclonic wind
and its lashed branches flail in the shrill black air
and the whole of heaven eddies with laceration
while under the skreegh of wind the herdsman hears
acorns pittering the rain-pocked soil
with palpitant volleys, gatling-gravel-pings,
so Dicie heard, from deep inside her skull,
how the tormenting third molar grunted, squeaked,
then twitter-stumbled like a stub of chalk
scraped across a blackboard to a shriek,
and she blubbered as the thick-embedded roots
tore at her gums till all at once,
with a popping suck it clopped into the dish
and rattled there, long-rooted, flung to defeat,
like Thestor when the quick
Patroclus hooked him down to black
Acheron and the terrible darkness came upon his eyes.
'Some alveolar mutilation...,' droned the Doc.
(Tenderly his left hand brushed her throat!)

The cruelty of remembered Greek
came to her help. Grammar, that
propriety of all well-measured speech,
comforted even the mouth too torn to speak.
Didn't our Lord cry out on Golgotha?
Only language stood against
the unimaginable savagery
of gods unable to imagine pain.

'Your courage... Extraordinary,' mumbled Diore.
He thought of inviting Dicie for a sleigh-ride,
he bent to kiss her hand but she,
she dismissed him, cowed him, with a curt
inclination. Shaking she gathered up
her reticule. She smoothed her bloody skirt.
She would not loose a cry for all the world
though her whole body howl. She swayed,
struggled to say, 'I thank you, Doctor,' but
it came out thickly as *Ah fank yu, Dagga...*
(Hopelessly, aflame with lust, he stood...)

True, in her pain she'd longed to roar
You base tooth-carpenter! and damn his eyes –
but this would have been ignoble, *infra dig,*
utterly at variance with what's decorous.
The doctor bowed and she bowed back to him.
I'd rather die than let
my suffering occasion a discourtesy.
What would we mortals be without propriety?
Swoopingly he held the door for her.

Precarious in hero as in suffragette,
Propriety is terror turned to etiquette.

The Jewel Box

For Norm Sibum

I have not done with you, I have not done,
Dear Presences, who live on in the spun
braids of gold in the silk jewel box, who glance
at me from clumsy cameos, who dance
out of lurid corals or a split earring,
whose throats I summon to the supple string
where the oily pearls of buried evenings burn,
whose flesh I taste on my own lips in the sleek
surfaces of onyx or the bleak
blurred filigree some dutiful son brought back
from the gold-sellers' souk, the lightning-crack
in the brooch.

I have not done with your memories
who wreathe around me still, whose reveries
would smother me, dear loving vampires
whom imagination and my own desires
conjure out of gems and gold and paste.

Our ancestors are stronger than the taste
of some abandoned attar we still find
back of the jewel box where sweet shadows wind
remembrance out of fragrance until our tongues
burn like the first air breathed into newborn lungs.

III

For a Modest God

For Karin Solway

That fresh towels invigorate our cheeks,
That spoons tingle in allotted spots,
That forks melodeon the guested air,
That knives prove benign to fingertips,
That our kitchen have the sweet rasp of harmonicas,
That stately sloshings cadence the dishwasher,
That lobsters be reprieved in all the tanks
And mushrooms fetched from caverns to the light
And that the oil of gladness glisten down
The chins of matriarchs, anoint the crib;
That there be aprons of capacious cloth
Enveloping the laps of nimble chefs,
That our sauces thicken on the days of fast,
That the hearth cat frisk his whiskers and attend,
That no domestic terror smite our minds,
That midnights be benignant with a god's
Oven mitts and spatulas and solace-broths:

A little god, a little modest god,
A godkin in a shriven cupboard, Lares-
Palmable and orderly, presiding
Over the hierarchies of the silverware,
Our platters' strata and our serving spoons;
A small mild god, ignorant of thunder,
Attuned to nothing more sombre than the trills
When all our crockery trembles to the fault
Of obscure, dimly rumorous calamities.

What the Snow Was Not

The snow was not liver-spotted like a gambler's
Hands. It did not reflect
Violet abrasions at the hubs of wheels
Or the well-glossed ankles of policemen.

The snow did not mimic flamingo rookeries
Or bone-stark branches where the spoonbills nest.
It had no single tint when it negated gold.
The snow was not duplicitous like arc

Lamps at sunrise that encairn the curbs
In lavender melodics. Snow did not web
The hands of women with their sudden hair
Electric-trellised in a blue downdraft.

The snow did not consume the eager mouths
Of children. It did not inhabit the skimming owl's
Concavity of surveillance and it did not flock
In grackle-shadows near the eaves of courts.

When you endow the snow with what it's not –
Mere shivering crystals blown by January
Over the squares in frosty negatives –
The snow becomes a god and nothing's lord.

Salle des Martyrs

You see where blessed Théophane was nailed
To a ceremonial plank in mockery
Of the crucifix he brought benighted souls
And how expertly the Mandarin's men sawed
His anointed limbs, one by one, away. It is
The love, in these depictions of
His mutilations, which most horrifies.
Wherever mere agony fails to persuade,
Some clumsy, well-meant brush stroke puddles
The dipped blood. His silken slippers
Discolour in the reliquary
Darkness of the Martyrs' Room, among
Pyx, monstrance, and ciborium, the
Golden home of the shriek.
He wrote, 'Only the weak
Are winnowed out for martyrdom.'

We stare at his stark remains under glass –
His thongs and worm-riddled breviary,
His rosary with all its silvery
Decades yet intact. And here, in a nearby
Case beneath the gravelly loudspeaker, we
May find the instruments we used to use
On one another: the rust-serrated words,
The garotte of indifference, the swords
Of our separate nights, the grudging thumb-
Screws of speechlessness, and that so slow
Obliviating boot that grinds out love.

No tableaux will commemorate our loss,
No delicate daubs of calligraphy our crown.
The pre-recorded messages wind down.
Beyond the blood-freckled alb and chasuble
An eighteenth-century Christ, all ivory,
Fissures upon His cross.
And outside, in the moist Parisian noon,
The rosebushes draw their redness from this room.

Mutanabbi in Exile

For Herb Leibowitz

In alien courts I melodied for bread
But now the sordid business of verse
Enjoins me to this dry northern
Kingdom where disaffected ostriches
Snort at sundown and the prince
Idles the hours away with paradigms
In ancient grammar books.

A shabby gentility obscured my youth.
Poverty was a stench I couldn't scrub
And largesse smarted out of others' hands.
But language was immeasurable as shame
And burned in the beatific mouth of God –
He is exalted! – and now language flows
From my fingertips and from my quill
The way the spider tessellates its silk.

My heart is fringed with arrows like the sun
Or the chastened, wincing surface of a blade
Hammered in Damascus out of Indian steel.
My heart is like the chilly ramparts of cranes
Longing southward as the winter dawns.
But my lines still rustle lovely as the slide
Of rosaries of olive wood blessed by pilgrimage
Or the pages, startled as acacia,
In the whispering codices of the Law.

The moon enacts its faded casuistries
And there are thorn trees twisted like beggars
By the last stones of encampments, the dry
Dung of pack animals, and *thumam* grass
Stuffed in the fire crevices. There I stopped
And all my pain swept over me
In that smooth-blown place.
How could such meagre anonymous shreds
Summon remembrance in a spill of tears?

South of Aleppo, where the stony mesas gust
With desolation and the jackal bitch whimpers
And snuffles in an unloved earth, my longing
Rang as hungry as the crows of winter.
The inkwell knows me, and the carven quill,
And the tense and crackling surfaces of parchment,
And swords and lances know me, and the strong horses,
And the night will remember me, and all empty places.

The Caliph

The wily and flamboyant Fatimid,
The intricate Caligula of God,
The neurasthenic delegate of prophets (may
God pray for them!), forbade all women
To wear shoes. He barred the cobblers from
Tapping their lasts or battering their little anvils;
Only poor prosodists could mime their hammer taps.

This, before he vaporised in the mauve
And umber desert of the air: al-Hakim,
Defender of the devious
Ambiguity of the Godhead, His penchant for
Bagatelles, creator of the paradox
Of sharks and swans, Draconian Comedian!

He placed an interdict on
Lamentation. He forbade all women to
Weep at funerals, rescinded ululations,
And so each black cortège
Wound through the lanes of Cairo voicelessly.
Even sorrow is too great a liberty
Since it inhabits memory, citadel
Beyond the fists of despots, or of God.

And sometimes, in the pitch-light of the bazaar,
God's shadow baited bears or egged men on
To braggadocio or fisticuffs, or spied upon
Their most secretive gestures, their least
Askance innuendoes, their cupped whisperings;
Till, surrogate, he evanesced on the Muqattam Hills
One evening, leaving only slivered veils behind.

Perhaps only the forbidden know
The unshod deprivations of the dead,
And perhaps only children who've just learned to walk
Savour the nakedness of heels and soles.
Perhaps only the mad
Value the little freedom of the shoes.

Lazarus in Skins

After his long recovery, Lazarus
Began wearing lizard–skin boots.
He sported cravats of rich kid
And black lustrous jackets of young calf.
He couldn't endure the cling
Of fabric, the insinuations of silk.
Even textiles woven of moth–soft cloth
Aggravated his dreams.

Not suffering, he said, but hope
Had made him hysterical and vain.
Now he desired the sinuous
Space of other skins, those fresh
Folds of amplitude, the beautiful
Blueness of snakes' eyes, cloud
Lenses, when they shed their last skin.

Forgetful Lazarus

Lazarus forgot his gloves and the blots
On his numb fingers showed too white.
He forgot the injustices of his shoes,
The lichens on his toes began to glow.
Lazarus could not remember to cover his mouth,
The grey smell of his entombment coiled out.

He also forgot his skyblue-tinted lenses
That made his sunken eyeballs shine with life.
He forgot to scrape away his death
That laced his arms and legs, his cheeks
– vivid and difficult as the rose-rich gills of fish –
with delicate ruffles of fungus, with sweet mould.

Lazarus and Basements

Lazarus had been a sluggish kid,
Fond of musky crevices where moles
Doze or where opossums paw their sour
Disreputable nests. He loved
That asylum of old clothes where moths
Webbed the spotted lightbulb or the crawl
Cellar where the fat exterminator went
On his monthly trips.

                At night he saw
Spiders in his sleep and dream itself
Furled outward in tough silk from the sly
Spinnerets of sleep. When he died,
They planted him in a damp and mildewed hole.
His basement nature had come home at last.

Imagine our surprise
Not at his wet, still-bandaged face
By the grave's low door,
Nor at the rank and vicious stink
That smoked from his shroud,
But at his loving familiarity with the damp
And the companionable clasp of his arms
Brimming with vermin
And all the grey caresses of his twittering friends.

Lazarus Listens

The relentless waltzes of the Golden Age
Retirement Club upstairs left him no peace.
All night their scything strings rippled his nerves,
Attuned to spider-sighs and beetle-whisperings.
All night he heard parades
And festivals, fiestas where rude shoes
Finessed their sad mazurkas into dawn.
And then, at dawn he heard the pure
Arpeggios of hooligans in stairwells
Or his ears, pitched
To the yawns of moths,
Followed the thin, self-conscious lullabies
Of senile women in their flowered chairs,
Cradling the surprise of light.

He was inert as earth,
Simple as sand, consummate as clay,
The driest obstacle, the echo-nest,
Against which all their music dumbly beat.

Mrs Lazarus

Believe me, it isn't easy
Even in a king-size bed
To sleep with the living dead.
You think I can enjoy
Buttering his morning toast
When the butter's not so cold as his grey ghost?
And he's always so theatrical:
'Honey, what I've been through!'
I say, 'Be a little stoical.
You could be lying in that sleazy
Mausoleum. Instead, you're here. With me.'

And let me tell you straight,
It's no mean trick to stimulate
A man like that
Fresh from a grimy grave:
He needs a paramedic just to shave.
At night his chilly skin
Sweats like a ripening cheese
And little bits keep dropping off
Till the poor guy's scared to sneeze.
And the pills, the specialists, the life supports!
There's even Streptomycin in his shorts.

I don't like the way he sits and squints
Or tilts off to one side in his La-Z-Boy.
Wouldn't you think he'd have a few small hints
For the living? Instead he whimpers *Ach!* or *Oy!*
'Honey,' is all he says, 'it wasn't Vegas!'

All night I smell his interrupted death.
It's my own individual hell.
All night I hug his contagious
Carcass dripping with verminous breath.
I calm him as he dreams and squirms.

I who adore Chanel
Now lie down with worms.

Hate

Hate is so bracing and accommodates
insight cosily. Hate icicles
the eyes. A happy hate rejuvenates,
gladdens hair, pinks the cheeks, bicycles
nimbly with the gusto of unchagrined exuberance.
An heirloom hatred's fun as well, accretes
in limestone ziggurats of bane. Hate lets you dance
on your own bones at last, and hate secretes

warm poisons, lovely but so lonely
venoms that pretext a hidden wish.
Obverse snugness of hate is only
like love in that it's not squeamish
at all; grasps in a rush, with sleek grace:
to mangle – or to caress – the other's face.

Gravediggers' April

In winter we comfort our dead with talk.
We entertain them with our idle gossip.
We whisper the news while our breath freezes.
We line up at the storage shed where their bodies lie
Awaiting the great thaws of uncertain spring.
We tell them how the frost was dark this year
And steep, how business perked up at the quarries,
What happened to those botanists after the avalanche...

The padlock on their door is lumpy
With a blackened ice
But our damp spurts of breath revive
The grieving hinges. Murmurous petals of frost
Cloud the numbed metal.
                                And quicker now,
More hurried, as the whisperers file
Behind the convenience store:

It's comforting to chat even if
No answers return. The winter shapes our words.
The widower drinks, the widow squeezes shut
Her eyes, imagining the bluish stain
Corruption spreads across a loved complexion.
Come back! they whisper, *I'm lonesome here without you!*
But then, as the winter drags, *I'm glad you're there
At last... where I can love you finally...*

Beyond the door they lie
Snug in their salt till spring. Some prefer
The new crematory in Schenectady but for most
Of us winter is unthinkable without
The long peace of our conversations.

In April, when the gravediggers return,
Staggering, soused to the gills, on overtime,
And the black lock thaws into rusty rain
And they bear them out through the open shed
Into the flowering cemetery,

Then we can mourn.

Nose

The nose is antithetical. It sniffs,
Snuffles, wallows in sneezes, then recoils
In Roman nobility, profile-proud;
Pampers its fleshy shadow in bas
Reliefs or is serenely alcoved within
Rotundas where the chiselled light
Dapples its expansive flanges.

                                    Nose
Is tuberous, root-like, with subsoil
Affinities, has its own mossy
Aromas, feels bulbous as corms or
Crimped as rhizomes; but even so,
Stands graced with little wings above
The harboured nostrils.

                               The nose
Sunders the face in symmetry,
Bisects us in hemispheres where selves
Negotiate along the boundary lines
Of smiles or scowls.

                            All night,
In the snug bed of the face,
The nose exults.

Fingernails

It is the patrimony of reptiles, or of birds,
To possess such pale claws, to sport such
Little flashes of keratin at the farthest tip
Of the grasp. The baby hoatzin has archaic
Claws along its barbarous wings
That boost it into the Peruvian trees;
So, too, our reminiscent hooks
That let our fingertips negotiate
The air, and that curve around so
Obediently, like shields at rest, with
All the snug patience of a carapace,
Snail's armature, or the fastidious
Hermit crab's limping pagoda of shell.

The manicurist lovingly rebukes
The creeping cuticle so that the faint
Crescents, like clouds along horizons,
Reappear. The fingernails are suffused
With the blood's sweet light
Though the nails of the newly dead
Possess a terrible hailstone
Opacity. The fingernails palisade
The unruly ranks of our wilful fingers
And whenever we clasp our hands,
A brief convivial darkness sheathes our nails.

Fetish

After we came home from the Exhibition
I felt drawn to make a figure out of wood.
I took a bulgy anonymous chunk, with bark
Attached and gummy tears near the frequent knots.
First I hacked and chopped; an anger
Somehow welled up, impelled my hands.
But the rough bristling form emerged:

Its hands were fingerless fists,
Its feet were lopped blocks.
Gently I gouged its bellybutton out and then
The face took its terrible shape –
That knobby lump of grieving watchfulness.
I suggested breasts and nipples
With red pegs. But then, as though instructed,
I modelled a fierce priapic flair,
Instinct with secret seed, double as snail-sex.

But the mouth's awe
Oppressed me – that torn place that prayed…
Upstairs I heard dinner and the gameshows begin.
Beyond the basement windows, rain prepared.
I had before me such a crooked god
Huge in the spotted bulb. So I took nails,
The shiny wide-head wood-nails from a keg,
And drove them skreaking home. Each spike
Increased its light, each hammer blow spilled
Adoration on the hunching thing, and I –
I knelt down before it while my lips burned.

My fetish swelled against its blinking nails,
Assumed a crabbed magnificence: *My pain had form.*
Its chopped mouth mirrored darkness: cascades
Of mirrors reflected an infinitude of dark,
Night within multiple night.

And then it spoke:

With upheld beggar's stumps *Bend down*, it said,

Bend down
And cherish me!

Blood

For Dan and Chuck

1

All night in your ears you'll hear the blood sing
I am king!   I am king!   I am king!

You'll hear the ganged hammers of the blood erect
Its palaces. You'll feel the sluices of the blood connect

Its empires. Blood with its royal, rotten scent,
In its rush-lit vestments, in its vehement

Arabesques, dangles its scarlet manacles
Or glows like radium inside sly ventricles.

In stables where no saviour lays his head
Blood shows its Balkan, its Rwandan, red.

Blood is apodictic in its contradictions,
Cascades from Adam's heart the crimson fictions

Of tribes and clans and families;
Knots the sinews with hot pieties.

2

Children not of my blood but of my love,
Whose sweet sonship is compounded of

All that mutual breath could make of hours,
We have plaited together what is ours

Minute by minute. Consanguinity
Knows nothing of our fierce fragility.

Blood relies
Hysterically on old school ties

While our enlacements all have been made
Thread by thread, braid upon braid.

3

When lawyers with their starry
Writs and decrees of certiorari

Banter your nativity,
Haggling some clotted pedigree,

Say, Blood should be slow, be slow,
Sound chuckle-melodic in heart's bungalow,

Be the hearthstone brightened by rich hemagogues,
The murmurous marrow of soft synagogues.

Let the vessels' cantillations in your throat
Dulcimer the temples' pulsing note.

For necklaces of ancestors twine love knots of time.
Backward to Eden let our recognitions rhyme.

Another Thing

To live in the body like a nervous guest;
To be confined in fingers and in feet;
To swing on the pendulum of what to eat;
To be subject to south and east and west...

Behind my skullbone lives another thing
That fidgets anxiously as I barge by,
That swivels skyward its chameleon eye
For the interest in the twitches of a wing.

My inmost dweller is predacious root;
Ransacks reality for steadfastness;
Adores the constancy of all dark stars;
Refuses thirst and thrives upon the brute
Benedictions of the wolf and lioness;
Loves the futility of fountains; preens scars.

Conquests of Childhood

North of a bottlecap lay Samarqand.
With pocketknives we divvied up the spoils.

With lances made of windshield wipers or of broken brooms
We hunted mighty Yazdegird to earth.
We cut his kingly throat, we stuck his head
On a creaking gatepost where his satraps stood.

East of a punctured inner tube there burned
The brazen furore of Heraclius.

West of the blear-eyed aggies in their pungent bag
We brought the terrible Berbers underfoot
And sailed on matchbox triremes through the Straits.

South of a slingshot made of forking twigs
And held together by a twanging band,
We saw the archipelagos of the newborn day
And unimaginable peoples coursing there.

Beyond the tyre pit Ecbatana shone.

Childhood Pieties

I grew up sullen, nervous, full of tricks.
St Paul and Milton were familiar ghosts.
I sniffed First Disobedience from the bricks
And mildewed plaster of the Lord of Hosts;
From smiling lies rouged with a crucifix;
The naphtha'd parlour and the Sabbath roasts;
The bitter bibles where the saved would mix
Apocalyptic gossip with their boasts.

I smirked rebellion and wet my bed.
Even the lustre of their sheets was fraud.
At nightmare time their Saviour, leeched with sin,
Crept in beside me, worming through my head,
Embraced me, stroked me, kissed me while I clawed
The frogcold mouth of jesus on my skin.

The Song of the Whisk

My flail demolishes
The gold of yolks;
My mesh abolishes
What it would coax.

The waterspout can frisk
While it soufflés the sea;
What's the twister but a whisk
For instant entropy?

I will erect a pinnacle
Of undulant béarnaise;
With clicketing quite clinical,
Paradisal mayonnaise.

Episode with a Potato

I was skinning a potato when it said:
Please do not gouge my one remaining eye!
My parer hesitated. The knob of the spud
Comforted my hand-hold with its sly
Ovoid, firm yet brittle as a fontanelle,
And I much enjoyed the way its cool lump –
All pulpy planes and facettings, with a starch
Sheen that mildly slimed my fingers
(Not to mention that tuberous smell
That lingers
Like the shoulder of a clump
Of creosote bushes or the violet mildew of an arch
No triumph still remembers) –
Yes, I liked the way it occupied my pinch.

I understood at its tiny squeak
The power of potentates over the members
Of their entourages. For a week,
Whenever I passed, the potato would flinch.
Its one eye never slept.
I thought of the kingdoms it had crept
Through under the ground, spud-
Smug, amid the dust of the bones of shahs
And eunuchs, those generations of the Flood,
The Colossi and the Accursed,
The Great Hunger and the hegiras,
Telemons and ostraca and, worst,
Immense anti-archives of dirt.

It hurt
Me to do it but I scooped out its eye
And ate it and felt utterly triumphant: I
Ingested all a potato could personify.

IV

Bavarian Shrine

In memory of Albert E. Flemming

1

The rusted feet of Christ in roadside shrines
Where the eager nail has bled into the stone
Transform the tough-hewn birch that disciplines.

His agony is fossilised in red
Lichens of corrosion on pale linden wood.

The oldtime craftsmen carved Him like a goose
With slathered ribs that spew out lymph and pus;
Three lurid ulcers colonise His thigh;
Pustules of malachite surround each eye.
A loving laceration smears His mouth.
Affection and the brute regard for truth
Suture His temples with the maggot's twist.
The black iron spikes surge from His wrists.

And yet, for me, this victim, tethered like
A swan, is lewd and holy:
                                        O Thou
Peacock of decay...

2

The spotted hogs trot past to the abattoir.
Their flanks are mired with fear-dung, and they squeal.
Their pink noses snuffle the poignant air.
Men club the hogs with black padded hammers,
Then swing them up on hooks and stab their throats.
Their shrieks are inconsolable and mad.
Their eerie voices give the shrine its cry.
Pilgrim, you shudder, stung by hurt and fear.
The thighs of Christ are burnished and severe.
A murderous perfection lights His eye.

A downy princess texture to the skin
— Only the exquisite can savour pain —
The royal exclamations of a flame
That feeds most fiercely on the tutored nerve.
Aristocratic in His gilded Calvary
— Did the numb peasants worship in His form
The hated bodies of their feudal lords,
Imagining beneath the ermine cloaks
Flesh that could whimper to the flail's white strokes?

3

The pretty little hogs with spotted sides,
Their fern-like ears scrolled over clever eyes,
That pick a delicate path on trotting hooves
Across the trash and mud of a weathered sty,
Enthralled me as I knelt beside the shrine.
(I share the German fondness for their swine.)

In autumn, when they come to butcher them, I
Memorise their long, despairing squeals
That fill the Bauernhof. I smell their blood,
The stink of singeing bristle and the smoke,
But feel the most for those that cannot cry,
Who wedge their frightened bodies to the fence
And shake with dumb-struck terror, paralysed
And staring, or expel quick spurts of nervous dung
That stains their patterned haunches and stiff tails.

And afterwards, just past the killing-ground,
I watched a hunting spider trap the flies
Invited by the reek of thickened blood;
Her dust-embedded web only an instrument,
All wonder butchered, pure function manifest,
With jags of dark heart's blood snagged on the strands.

Railyard in Winter

The colours of disused railyards in winter;
the unnamed shades of iron at four o'clock;
the sun's curiosity along abraded stones;
corrosion that mimes the speckled lichen of woods;
the islands of stubbly rust on padlocked doors;
the fierce shoots of winter grass among cinders;
the fragile dim light, infused with tannin,
that falls clear on the stamped bottle-glass
and regales the castoff boot.

                The colours of shale
cratered with dark rain. The rough knots
of crabgrass near the steps to the loading dock
and their sandy scruffed umber.

                The hues
of all negligible things: the nugatory blue
of slagchunks between the ties. Then, the smell
of those resinous blisters of red on the fence,
like a childhood of pines.

                Such unpeopled places
luxuriate on Sundays. What was made for use
discloses in uselessness its transient magic;
assumes the radiance of the useless grasses.

Florida Bay

A flittering of breeze, so hesitant,
Rustles my face before the sun is up,
So subtle that it seems the diffident
Touch of my children's fingers on my cheek.
I sit there with a wobbly coffee cup
Cocked on one drowsy knee. For over a week
This tender, pre-dawn breeze has signalled day.
It blows here from the south, from Florida Bay,

Where Florida curves westward to the Gulf,
The continent's dead-end, our Finistère.
If you turn inward now to find yourself
As you once were, you will ignore that breeze
With its humid scent of flowers. There,
In the brightening room old recollections tease
And elude you in forgotten things
While morning flickers with premonitory wings.

I used to wonder why I felt so out,
Not seeing that it was my mulish nature.
And now, at fifty, when I've just about
Finished with childhood (though dissatisfied),
The child's desolation, his nomenclature
Of loneliness, projected and identified
With the furniture of Sunday dining rooms
After the pot roast and the macaroons,

Still so possesses me.
                        And though we leave
The darkness of their tears behind the door,
Shut our ears to their cries, refuse to grieve
For those we hated with the force of love,
Their desperation not to be forgotten or
Forsaken follows us till we are victims of
Every laceration of their breath
That will not leave us even in their death.

And desolation will always be those warm
Miami afternoons when August rain
Accumulated in the distance, before the storm
Amassed and broke, and plump drops lashed
The tattered fronds outside, or hurricane
Roared from Tortugas north with stillness stashed
Inside its eye, and we waited for the wind
To flay the stucco and leave the banyan skinned.

Waiting, waiting – childhood solitude
Of toys in the moted morning sun –
O intimations of a requiem. The mood
Befell me like the sweet metallic tune
Of a Sunday carousel before the ride is done,
That sense of perpetual and soon-
To-be-cherished happiness... Remember your surprise
At the candled mirrors that returned your eyes

In diamond encirclings till you'd spot
An icicle kaleidoscope of yourself
Amid the ponies' melodious trot,
And think, Is that me? Is that my face?
As though a stranger lent you a strange self
That stared back at you from the secret place
Mirrors rise out of, or the near-familiar look
Of photos of cousins tucked in an old schoolbook.

Remember the smell of the hall bookcase?
Inside the little mullioned panes that held
Embrittled paperbacks, you saw your face
Compromised by shadows and were scared,
While with a smudging fingerprint you spelled
The titles of the books in French or stared
At foxed engravings in the *Illustrated*
London News, its fashions of the celebrated

Looking so weird in the Miami light,
The roach-specks and the spider-silk impressed
With long-squashed rosebuds in a tome clapped tight
For decades. And dead cousin Arthur's photograph,

His First Communion suit, his parents dressed
In ascots and in flounces, a pleased faint laugh
Beginning at the corners of his mouth,
Among shrill memorabilia of the South:

Taffeta bows, a dance card, a leather purse
Embossed Havana, steamship souvenirs,
Pearl opera glasses, scraps of verse
In coffee-coloured copperplate, a lock of hair,
Child's hair, beribboned, and the quaint gold shears
That snipped it, in a reticule. Aware
Even then of the poisons of the past,
You touched these keepsakes warily at the last.

Is there where desolation began?
In that artifice of intimacy
I suffered then? I was the 'little man',
The fragile simulacrum of the male
Swaddled in fisticuffs and mock gentility.
I puffed a self out on the sail
Of my matchbox boat that skimmed the pond,
Its makeshift mainstay bowing as it swanned.

You'll know mementoes by their bandages,
Their plush and tissue gauzes: safe from life!
They are embowered like the unopened pages
In those old volumes you would puzzle over,
Their signatures uncut by the curious knife
And only dreamy fade-marks on the cover.
But in the end I'll pack the books away
And go outside, drive south, toward Florida Bay

Where the peninsula, above the Keys,
Opens into an unimpeded view.
There once I saw the white birds from their rookeries
Of bobbing islands clatter up and fly
And though I cling to memory, as if I knew
Devotion were fiercer than that wing-divided sky,
I'll bow before them as they skim the ground:
Outside ourselves is where our selves are found.

Daybreak at the Straits

I bow to your divinity who created darkness before creating light.

Ethiopic hymn (author unknown)

In memory of Richard Outram

1

The clouds that lie in cinnabar striations
are juggled by a nimble waterspout
too distant for significance. The dim
pink of daybreak binds the sky with dark
barely distinguishable from a darker sea.
The horizon mortices itself with chinks of rose.
What we call day is nothing more
than disintegrated darkness at the Straits.
Night bickers for asylum still
in unlaced shoes, implores the paling windowpanes
to be steadfast for dark against the light.
I am witness to the spectral provocations
daylight introduces to a vista
that all night stood
islanded by nothing but the stars.

2

Tired of the meditations on futility
that now retard my nights I walked to see
the waters of the Straits in darkness hesitate,
recoil and hover, tremble just before they calibrate
shocked sandstone, the staved cliff, the pitiable
barricades we raise against the terrible
erosions waves exact. The wind's a whittler here,
pares quartz to thinnest splinters, loves the sheer
spare sea-lathed skeletons of objects cast ashore.

It comforts me at night, a watchman of the stars
that only change by reasonable laws, to parse
the luminous degradations of the dark
as lethal light insinuates and tinges. Dogs bark
down at Rice Point, a rooster clears its throat outside.
From the cliff a cormorant topples like a suicide.

3

In the watches of the night, as the Psalmist said,
I meditate on darkness, I remember my dead.
The dark is palpable, has a silken-sash-drawn feel,
gloves the troubled fingertips with a cochineal
comfort, the way spring water laves the skin
with its brisk, plush touch. I will gather in
my hours as the darkness climbs and spreads.
It has become the ocean. Up to our heads
we bob and drift, remembranceless,
and for all we cling to spars of nothingness,
names burn their starlight on dark irises.

I feel the soul inside me, dear diaeresis
that thews my breath and flesh, that separates
heart's thrusting muscle as it meditates
from all the rough heart cherishes, I sense
the supple disjunctions of the animal
threshed in the indiscernible
meshes of the element and, terrified,
crow with the cock and bark with the farmer's dog,
wriggle awake, crawl from the salt bog
of sleep unsatisfied:

on my lips and on my eyelids as the new
sun shoulders the clouds aside,
a darkness sits, intangible as dew.

A Salt Marsh near Truro

The wind has rubbed the dead trees to a shine
And now it flattens all the grasses down
To cowering bundles, slick and serpentine,
That twist and curtsey by the muddy brown
Brink of the salt marsh with its alkaline
Tinctures that transfigure what they drown.
The trees form a writhy circle with their brine-
Burnt branches hooked up like the six points on a crown.

Gnats and midges, the fumes of raw methane,
That oily sun going down along the Bay,
Veiled in bright pollutants, and the wind
Eroding everything to its low plane,
Convince you that this marsh of hot decay
Leaves nothing newborn that has not been skinned.

Nova Scotia

The topography is of slight relief, and innumerable lakes, streams, bogs,
barrens and stillwaters occur.

Flora of Nova Scotia (1945)

For David Solway

Here, south of Halifax, near Peggy's Cove,
Where the coastline shoulders out into the sea,
You search the landscape for its difficult
Splendour. There are sudden gullies and domes
Littered with glacial boulders in a jagged
Equipoise. The glacier's nosing wedge
Dishevelled all the hillsides and the stones
Seem sprinkled by a child. Gargantuan
Spills of granite balance on dainty
Hillocks and the mauve arroyos
Have a stunned and smoky look
Like gaping survivors of some detonation.

Each thing seems hieroglyphic to your eye.
Tough decumbencies of spurge
Thicken the glance. The cheeks of rocks
Are bearded with lichens in rough,
Persistent whorls. Sometimes in a crevice
Of the cast-up rock you'll come upon
Improbable orchids or a bullfrog croaks
From one of the many little pools of rain
Skittered by windblown spray. Maybe you'll find
Fragments of shell and glass that have
The cadence of the North Atlantic in their
Sleek, barbaric shapes. But
The narrow pathway twists between
Contiguous desolations, indifferent
To history, and there is
The momentary, quickly avoided sense
That all we cling to here is scaffolding
Above slashed granite and the ocean's voice.

You won't sing hymns to seals
Along the sharp immersions of this coast
Nor will you drink transfiguring
Mouthfuls of the pure and bitter wind
From your chill chapped hands.
But maybe there your moment will arrive
Unaccompanied by memory
Or expectation and you'll see
Simply what lies before you or ahead,
Observe it with a purgatorial
Precision of the eye,
And speak it in the justice of the tongue.

Later, beyond the coastline you will come
Out of season to the dark hotel
Where your room overlooks the sea.
The gaudy awnings will be rolled up for the spring,
The seaward patio swept bare, the hulls
Of summer's pleasure boats aligned
And tarpaulined, and maybe there will be
A single lantern with its oily light
Reflected in the ocean of November.
There in your seclusion from the wind
All night in dreams of home you'll listen for
The cold companionship of distant waves,
Hear squalls beating and the seethe of foam.
Abstracted from particulars, alone
With the uncertain fluttering of your breath,
You'll listen to rafters creaking and the clack of glass
And in the far-off vehemence of that darkness, still
Suspended between memory and hope,
All night you'll hear
The North Atlantic, just beyond the cove,
Banging its knuckles on the heartless sill.

Gazing at Waves

At Morbihan or Montauk or at Peggy's
Cove, or where the little drab cornice
South of Casablanca runs to sand,
Wherever there's an ocean promontory,
People always look far out to sea
As though expecting some unheard-of
Apparition to arise, beyond the waves
Where the horizon glitters like an eye
Peeping through a sleepy eyelid.

                    Why
Do they look so searchingly out there?
Do they think the sea can offer more
Than corrugated combers or
That queasy smell of peaches that the shore
Concocts from mussel shells and clumps of kelp?

Maybe there's satisfaction in the prompt
Pinnacles of waves, their tasselling
Symmetrical ascensions, and that sense
Precision amid pandemonium
Provides.

At other times, more rarely now perhaps,
Some little shiver of acknowledgement
Still finds us there
Between the stately troughings and the
Counterglides, the scattered plash
Of droplets, with the keen gulls
Mewing and the rocks
Reflective of a light too old for us,
And this gives back our
Littleness again, this restores
Some sort of privileged insignificance;
Or will the waves always appear mere
Sequent arrival without consequence?

The spectacle is sovereign, yet intimate.
How soon the waters enter our
Attention, follow us in sleep,
Accompany the cadence of our minds,
Seem punctual and seriatim, curled
In all the beauty of futility,
So promptly mortal as they gather in,
Ascend and hover in the gusting air,
Then amble over into hiddenness,
Fold themselves in sand like drowsy claws
Curved into the twilight of the nest.
Is it a consolation to be witnesses
Of what so lucidly evades our gaze?
Is gazing a favour that gazed waves bestow?

An Epistle from Rice Point

Nothing's gone smoothly at Rice Point. The cod
I cooked for lunch the other day had worms
And when I forked the fillet gingerly,
A fat and pinkish snout came writhing out.
My sons were sickened and quite off their feed
But I addressed the impertinence of squirms
That had enlaced our lunch with three
Brusque dollops of hot sauce. It flailed about
And finally it spoke, that worm, and said:

How dare you ladle sauce upon my head?
I am the abyssal worm that feeds
In darkness on the deep floor of the sea –
A tender coiling consciousness that breeds
In the fibres of the flesh, a wriggle-god,
A lithe mind that rivulets stupidity –
The lumpy and dull-witted race of cod...

'The cod was beautiful, and you are not,
You slimy eyeless annulated pest,'
I shot back and I brained it with a pot.
The worm came eeling back and now addressed
My dumbstruck sons:

                    At midnight I will twist
All through your nightmares. I'm the worm
The Gospel speaks of that will never die
And I dwell with the worm that dieth not
Inside your brainpans like a doubled fist.
Behind your foreheads where the bad dreams squirm
I'll snuggle up and peek out through your eye
Unless you eat me live.

                    I took the hot
Tip of my carving knife and chopped the talkative beast
In sections, but each inch curled and writhed,
A dozen cod-worms down the platter scythed
In a sort of Todestanz combined with jive.

We are the laily worms that haunt the sea
(the wormy segments piped in harmony).
We are envenomed with the dreams of reefs,
The lobsters' anxieties, the oysters' griefs,
The lachrymose neurosis of the eel,
The torpid Weltschmerz *of the cochineal...*

'Enough!' I thundered and switched on the Moulinex.
'I've had enough of this annelid hex!'
I sluiced the worm-ends in the canister,
Set it to *Mince* and then *Purée*, but faster
Than I could macerate those vocal segments
Their shrill harmonics rang in yammer fragments.
A soup of cod-worms gave a grand chorale
From the kitchen at Rice Point. My terrified
Teenagers watched the worm-broth swell,
Tentacular and spittle-crested, a pale pink tide
Of liquid parasitic cod-worm consommé
Engulfed us where we crouched. I cried, *Assez!*
We wolfed the worm-soup down with zealous spoons
And mopped up every drop. The taunting tunes
Have ended now for good. All is again well
Here by the ocean down at Rice Point.

Farewell... Farewell.

Coastlines

1

Barnacles cinch
Sea-battered pilings.
Dog whelks maraud in mud.
How the North Atlantic
Wrangles the rocks!
Above, the houses of the fishermen
Look matchstick but are fierce.
They hold to the skittish boulders with all their might.
Next door, in the wired-off
Graveyard of the cove,
The headstones lean aslant,
Scripture pages thumbed down by the wind.
Below them the ocean
Seethes and scathes all day,
All night, and the spray
Smokes where it slaps the shore.
Tide pools boil with foam.

On coastlines you realise
What world will last.
See how the lean light
Glances against granite.
Erosion gorges the coastline out,
Nibbles the gaps.
You feel a shiver in
The ocean's memory.

2

What if this coastal road, these roofs
Vivid against the ocean, these
Steeples and these gas
Stations, what if these docks and piers and
Marinas, these tough
White houses with their windowboxes,
Stood only in the minute's multitude?
What if each minute made its universe?
What if in our hands we held our world
Breakable and rainbow-velveted as mere
Wobbling bubbles that our children blow?
I feel my skin, I feel my face,
Yield to the light as coastlines yield,
Accepting the loving
Phosphorescence of daylight's
Demarcation. I feel
The violence of all its delicacy.

3

Coastlines are where our opposites ignite
And no one can say, *After all, it's all right.*
Coastlines are where your father and your mother
Turn without a word forever from each other.
Coastlines are where the quick-footed sun
Touches Ultima Thule and can no longer run.
Coastlines are where we learn the ocean's tragedy:
Incessant endeavour, incessant panoply,
Broken down to crumbs of nothingness
And yet we want to bless
Each ragged repetition of the waves –

So inconsolable, so close to us.

An Oak Skinned by Lightning

The oak tree skinned by lightning is ringed round
With woodlice trails on its inmost bark.
The scars of the oak startle: each mark
Of its once-hid flesh revels in profound

Asymmetry our eyes must dote upon.
The random meanders of the blind woodlice
Cut their labyrinthine cicatrice
Of cryptic squiggles in soft cambium.

Their carved grooves look like staves and notes of scores
A cello ellipsoidally transmutes
Before the main theme flutters to the flutes.
I feel these clear canals. My fingers parse

These worm trails laid bare like epigraphy.
The oak was Christlike as the lightning stripped
Its seamless raiment off and the rain whipped
It while it shook, a suffering being, in July

When even dragonfly and hawkmoth seem benign.
I am moved by the incommunicable script
Of the lightning on the oak tree's swept
Pith. Is this the idiolect of summer, the sign

Our eyes are aching to decode,
These edicts from a cancelled chancery,
These mute communicados of the sensory,
Whose each jot seems a letter in a word?

My fingertips Champollion the oak;
The burined lice trails teach my skin.
Here hands alone, not eyes, draw you within
The secretive syllables the lightning struck.

The Public Gardens

The Public Gardens are so cunningly
Laid out. The boxwood has symmetrical
Barbarity of shape. And the walkway
With its fractal jaggedness dissuades
The eye. Linden colonnades will shine
Like faces at a solemn protocol
Brushed with tears. In November, the long line
Of the damp trees oppresses. The blades
Of the tall grasses spiral sinuously.
There is such a definitive edge to the border
Of the hoed-up beds. This is a place of order
Despite its delicate wilderness disarray.

Here, three years ago, I watched a swan
Trundle in a chicken-wire enclosure
Like something perishable stored up for the spring.
The swan looked muddy and obese.
Its horny, latex-coloured feet unnerved
Me. This was not the virile, ominous
Swan of Yeats, the gliding cynosure
Of all imagination. Only a close-docked wing
Remained of all that majesty. Beyond the wan,
Superannuated roses, brambled and brown-edged,
Full of some fear that I could taste, police
Cars by the black gates wetly reconnoitred
Where hunched unshaven men smoked and loitered,
And the festive statues, rain- and mildew-ledged,
Gestured spaciously with luminous
Fingers where the civic soot collected.

The swan brought back to mind a horrible
Thing I'd seen there once, a hungry seagull
Perched upon a half-dead mallard's back
And eating its raked and squirming flesh alive.
It might have been hideously symbolical –
The mystical amalgam of two beasts
In which the stronger on the weaker feasts –

But for the pitiful, writhing, bony neck
Of the injured duck. Its pain deflected
Darwinian pieties, too bland in any case to give
Individual significance to pain,
And I remembered how, some weeks before,
I'd eaten roast duck with a rich plum sauce.
Here was the flesh itself, with crass
Thrashings agonising, while the quick gull tore
Slivers of slitted skin and dabbled its bill again
In flinching meat.

              Pain estranges,
Cordons the sufferer and disarranges
Pity in its strict perimeters:
I thought of people I'd known, sufferers
So perimetered by pain that only love
Could touch them still – sometimes, not even love.

With a stick I chased away the gull above
And then I laid the stick along the torn duck's neck
And leaned until it broke with a little click
And both its wings fanned out reflexively,
Tremoring and hovering and an almost terrible
Exhilaration poured along my hands and arms,
Though I also felt the nausea you feel
When pain intrudes on beauty and disarms
The order obligatory for the beautiful,
And I knew how much I'd loathed that hurt bird
That had suffered so like me,
Or you, in muddy miserable twitches, wincingly.

I left the Public Gardens with its rows
Of neatly mattocked beds, I, a poet, one of those
Virtuosos of the nerves, and what had I seen,
Suppurative, shame-naked, and obscene?
In muted wards, some agony unwinds;
Beyond the still facades, behind Venetian blinds,
Some passion enacts its ritual
Desecration of the actual.
The horror in my mouth was almost prayer,

The stumbled syllables of those in despair,
And yet, so poetical, so apposite!
Does order merely gauze the infinite
Wince of the debrided skin? And was pity
Conferral of extinction or the first stone of the city
Founded in love?
That day, I saw the fountains with their casual
Music of refusal
Splash beyond while in its pen the great
Mud-spattered swan beaked its black gate.

History

This is our history.
The place is empty now where we began.
The rooms are full of sunlight and the sea
Effaces all the traces where we ran.

I dreamt about the world before I was,
That darkened curve of shore, the stark
Clarity of coral undersea. Does
Broken coastline demarcate the dark

Of unbeginning daylight? Now I see
The twining light with all the dark I can.
This is our history:
The place is empty now where we began.

Acknowledgements

I am deeply indebted to my friend the poet and essayist Marius Kociejowski who first suggested the present selection, chose the poems, arranged them in their present order and pressed the manuscript, with firm but delicate insistence, on the attention of Carcanet. And I am grateful to Michael Schmidt for his generous acceptance.

Individual poems first appeared in the following publications:

The Antigonish Review ('Starfish'), *Arc* ('Epistle from Rice Point'), *Arvon Foundation Anthology*, 1987 ('Bavarian Shrine'), *Blueline* ('History', 'Mullein', 'An Oak Skinned by Lightning', 'Railyard in Winter'), *Boston Review* ('Gravediggers' April'), *Chelsea* ('Fetish'), *Descant* ('Hate'), *The Fiddlehead* ('Rooster'), *Gastronomica* ('Episode with a Potato'), *The Gettysburg Review* ('Flamingos'), *Grand Street* ('Mutanabbi in Exile'), *Index* ('Gazing at Waves'), *Literary Imagination* ('A Salt Marsh near Truro'), *Maisonneuve* ('Cradle Song of the Emperor Penguins'), *The Malahat Review* ('The Baboons of Hada', 'Microcosm'), *Mockingbird* ('Nova Scotia'), *The New Republic* ('Anhinga', 'Origins'), *The Other Side* ('Skunk Cabbage'), *The Oxford American* ('The Crossing', 'Finding a Portrait of the Rugby Colonists'), *The Paris Review* ('Conquests of Childhood'), *Parnassus* ('What the Snow Was Not'), *PN Review* ('After Becquer'), *Poetry Ireland Review* ('Another Thing', 'Ant-Lion', 'Childhood Pieties', 'Dicie Fletcher'), *The Quarterly* ('Lazarus in Skins', 'Lichens', 'Spider'), *Shenandoah* ('Forgetful Lazarus', 'Lazarus and Basements', 'Lazarus Listens'), *The Southern Review* ('Florida Bay', 'Hand-Painted China').

The following poems first appeared in *The New Yorker*: 'Adages of a Grandmother', 'The Ant Lion', 'The Caliph', 'Childhood House', 'Conch Shell', 'Fingernails', 'For a Modest God', 'Garter Snake', 'Getting Ready for the Night', 'Grackle', 'My Mother in Old Age', 'Rain in Childhood', and 'The Song of the Whisk'. 'A Freshly Whitewashed Room' was accepted for publication in *The New Yorker* in 1993 but has yet to appear. *Vitae summa brevis spem nos vetat inchoare longam!*

All the poems have been published, often in different versions, in book form as follows:

Bavarian Shrine and other poems (Toronto: ECW Press, 1990)
Coastlines (Toronto: ECW Press, 1992)
For a Modest God (New York: Grove Press, 1997)
Araby (Montreal: Signal Editions, 2001)
Daybreak at the Straits (Lincoln, NE: Zoo Press, 2004)
Time's Covenant: New and Selected Poems (Windsor, ON: Biblioasis, 2007)

'Starfish', 'Skunk Cabbage' and 'Origins' were anthologised in *The Norton Anthology of Poetry* (New York: Norton, 1996, 4th edition; and 5th edition, 2005), edited by Margaret Ferguson, Mary Jo Salter and Jon Stallworthy. 'My Mother in Old Age' was included in *The Norton Introduction to Literature* (New York: Norton, 1991; 5th edition). 'Adages of a Grandmother' was anthologised in *Literature: The Human Experience* (New York: St Martin's Press, 1997). 'Rooster' was republished in *Fiddlehead Gold: Fifty Years of the Fiddlehead Magazine* (Fredericton, NB, 1995). 'Skunk Cabbage' and 'Live Oak, with Bromeliads' were included in *Flora Poetica: An Anthology of Poems about Flowers, Trees, and Plants* (London: Chatto and Windus, 2001), edited by Sarah Maguire. 'My Mother in Old Age', 'Adages of a Grandmother', 'Childhood House' and 'Getting Ready for the Night' have been anthologised in *Motherhood: Poems about Mothers*, edited by Carmela Ciuraru (New York: Everymans Library, 2005). 'Mutanabbi in Exile' was included in *Syria: Through Writers' Eyes*, edited by Marius Kociejowski (London: Eland, 2006; 2nd revised edition, 2010). 'The Caliph' is included in *Caliph of Cairo: Al-Hakim bi-Amr Allah, 996-1021*, by Paul E. Walker (Cairo; New York: The American University in Cairo Press, 2009). 'Episode with a Potato' has been anthologised in *The Gastronomica Reader*, edited by Darra Goldstein (Berkeley: University of California Press, 2010).

'The Song of the Whisk' was set to music for two voices and piano by Jed Feuer and released on the CD *twenty-one songs* (Feuermusic, 2002).